SYMPHONY OF THE GAME

DEEP HOOPS

LOUIS BARHAM

SYMPHONY OF THE GAME

Louis Barham
Symphony of the Game
All rights reserved.
Copyright © 2024 by Louis Barham

No part of this publication may be reproduced, distributed, or transmitted in any form or by any means, including photocopying, recording, or other electronic or mechanical methods, without the prior written permission of the publisher, except in the case of brief quotations embodied in critical reviews and certain other noncommercial uses permitted by copyright law.

Published by Spines
ISBN: 979-8-89383-470-3

CONTENTS

Acknowledgments — vii

1. The Power of the First Move: A Deep Dive into Basketball's Strategic Landscape — 1
2. Reading the Opponent's Cascades: A Strategic Symphony Unveiled: — 13
3. How the Game is Being Learned — 25
4. The Art — 31
5. Harmony — 43
6. The Basketball Meme Pool - A Symphony of Replication, Mutation, and Selective Pressures — 49

About the Author — 63
Untitled — 65
Untitled — 67

ACKNOWLEDGMENTS

To acknowledge Janus Sanders is an understatement. As we embarked on the seemingly impossible journey of converting an overtrained athlete into a technical professional, Mr. Sanders played a pivotal role. He became a profound translator for me, connecting emotions, feelings, and actions with words and information that I had not previously known. His guidance felt God-given. I am deeply grateful for his obedience and assistance. If you ask him, he will most importantly say that it was the Father who blessed him so he could bless me, and for that, we are both thankful. Because I didn't have to give one up for the other. I now possess both skills showed me that sacrifice wasn't needed, just a particular skill set of learning how to learn

CHAPTER 1

THE POWER OF THE FIRST MOVE: A DEEP DIVE INTO BASKETBALL'S STRATEGIC LANDSCAPE

IN THE REALM OF BASKETBALL, where the squeak of sneakers against the hardwood is a rhythmic heartbeat, and the cheers of the crowd echo like a symphony. Every move on the court is a brushstroke on the canvas of victory or defeat.

In this exploration, we embark on a journey to unravel the layers of "The Power of the First Move," a chapter that transcends the confines of the basketball court to become a manifesto for strategic thinking, mindfulness, and the profound impact of decisions.

Unpacking Action Cascades:

The narrative unfolds with the introduction of a pivotal concept — action cascades. Picture this: A player receives the ball and takes a split-second to decide whether to pass, dribble, or shoot. That singular decision becomes the catalyst, setting off a chain reaction of events that can sway the game's momentum.

Action cascades illuminate the dynamic nature of basketball, where one move is not an isolated incident but a domino that can topple the entire sequence of play.

As we delve deeper into this concept, it becomes apparent that the basketball court is not merely a stage for physical prowess; it is a strategic battlefield. The first move, once perceived as a mere initiation, now transforms into the opening move in a chess game where foresight, analysis, and precision matter.

Conceptualize. Your thoughts?

Significance of Every Move:

The stage is now set for appreciation of the importance of every move made on the court. Each dribble, pass, or defensive stance becomes a critical piece of the game's intricate puzzle.

Extended exploration unveils the layers beneath the surface, urging players to view their actions not as mere transactions within the game but as strategic investments in the team's success. Beyond the literal interpretation, the first move becomes symbolic, embodying the essence of strategic thinking.

The player, whether consciously or not, holds the power to shape the game's narrative. This extended narrative invites players to consider the weight of their decisions, fostering a sense of responsibility that transcends the immediate play in Real-Life Examples.

Conceptualize. Your thoughts?

The Tapestry of Basketball History:

To breathe life into these theoretical concepts, real-life examples emerge as the tapestry woven with the threads of basketball history. Anecdotes of legendary players making pivotal moves, altering the course of a game or even an entire season, are dissected. These stories become more than just reminiscences; they transform into valuable lessons, illustrating the tangible impact of the first move.

Consider the narrative of a buzzer-beater, where a player, against all odds, takes the shot that decides victory or defeat. The extended exploration of such moments serves as a testament to the enduring legacy of decisions on the court.

Young athletes are encouraged to draw inspiration from these narratives, recognizing their role not just in the present but as contributors to the sport's ongoing saga.

Conceptualize. Your thoughts?

Long-Term Consequences: Nurturing Mindfulness and Strategic Thinking:

The pivots, to nurture the seeds of mindfulness and strategic thinking among young athletes. The emphasis is not merely on the immediate consequences of a move but on the enduring impact it can have on the team and the individual player's journey.

The first move, once a fleeting moment, now becomes a juncture where young athletes are encouraged to pause, reflect, and consider the long-term ramifications of their decisions.

Mindfulness, often associated with meditation and being present at the moment extends its tendrils into the world of sports. The player is urged not just to react instinctively but to engage in a thoughtful and intentional decision-making process. The basketball court becomes a realm where mental acuity is as vital as physical prowess, and every move is a manifestation of a well-calibrated mind.

Conceptualize. Your thoughts?

Off the Court: Lessons Beyond Basketball:

"The Power of the First Move" extends beyond the boundaries of the court, prompting players to consider the broader implications of their decisions in the grand theater of life. Once confined to the constraints of a game, strategic thinking becomes a transferable skill, shaping not just the athlete but the individual navigating the complexities of existence. Decision-making becomes a holistic endeavor, whether on the court or in the broader context of life.

The player is invited to recognize the parallels between a well-timed pass and a calculated decision in a professional or personal setting. The extended narrative serves as a bridge, connecting the strategic landscape of basketball with the strategic challenges encountered beyond the court's boundaries.

Conceptualize. Your thoughts?

The Butterfly Effect of Decisions:

As we navigate through the chapters of basketball history, the butterfly effect of decisions becomes increasingly evident. A seemingly small action, akin to the flutter of a butterfly's wings, can set in motion a series of events that shape the destiny of a game. The extended exploration of this phenomenon deepens the player's appreciation for the interconnectedness of actions on the court.

Consider the scenario where a player's decision to intercept an opponent's pass not only disrupts their offensive play but also initiates a fast break, resulting in a crucial score. The butterfly effect, in the context of basketball, exemplifies how one decision, one move, can resonate far beyond its immediate impact from Solo Moves to Team Symphony.

The narrative gracefully transitions from solo moves to the symphony of the team. Action cascades, initially explored as individual decisions, now become a collective dance where every player contributes to the rhythm of play. The extended exploration underscores the importance of cohesion, communication, and coordination within the team.

The first move, while retaining its individual significance, is now perceived as a harmonious note in the collective melody of the team. Young athletes are encouraged to not only recognize their individual agency but to synchronize their moves with the broader strategy of the team.

The basketball court becomes a stage where individual brilliance finds its zenith within the harmonious orchestration of team play.

Conceptualize. Your thoughts?

The Emotional Quotient of Decisions:

In the expanded exploration, the emotional quotient of decisions takes center stage. Decisions on the court are not sterile transactions but emotional investments that can evoke joy, frustration, or resilience. The player is often viewed through the lens of statistics and strategy and is humanized in this extended narrative.

Consider the emotional rollercoaster of a player facing a critical decision in the dying moments of a close game. The extended exploration of the emotional resonance of decisions invites players to embrace the depth of their emotional engagement on the court. It emphasizes the intricate interplay between the mind and the heart, urging players to harness the emotional energy as a catalyst for strategic brilliance.

Conceptualize. Your thoughts?

Action Cascades in Opponent Psychology:

The exploration extends to the intricacies of opponent psychology in the face of action cascades. A perceptive player, through strategic moves, not only influences the dynamics of their team but can disrupt the opponent's mental equilibrium. The extended narrative becomes a playbook for understanding the psychological warfare inherent in basketball.

Consider the scenario where a player consistently makes successful drives to the basket. The opponent's defense adjusts, creating opportunities for perimeter shooters. The extended exploration of this strategic chess match between players and opponents unveils the layers of psychological maneuvering, where each move is a calculated gambit in the battle for dominance.

Conceptualize. Your thoughts?

The Art of Recovery: Bouncing Back from Setbacks:

No exploration of basketball's strategic landscape is complete without delving into the art of recovery. The extended narrative becomes a guide for players to navigate setbacks, emphasizing that the game is not defined solely by success but by the resilience displayed in the face of challenges. Consider a player missing a crucial shot in the closing seconds of a game. The extended exploration of recovery becomes a roadmap for current and future endeavors.

Conceptualize. Your thoughts?

CHAPTER 2

READING THE OPPONENT'S CASCADES: A STRATEGIC SYMPHONY UNVEILED:

IN THE INTRICATE dance of basketball, where every move is a note in the symphony of play, the ability to read and interpret the cascades in opponents' actions emerges as a defining skill.

This exploration delves into the realm of strategic insight, unraveling the tapestry of intellect and cascades that skilled players, coaches, and recruiters masterfully navigate.

As we embark on this journey, the court transforms into a chessboard, and the game becomes a mental battlefield where intellect and strategic play intertwine.

The Chessboard of Basketball:

Skilled players, coaches, and recruiters, much like seasoned chess players, possess the astute ability to anticipate and decipher cascades in opponents' actions. The basketball court becomes a dynamic chessboard, where moves are not just physical but strategic. Reading the opponent's cascades is akin to foreseeing the adversary's next move, understanding the patterns, and staying a step ahead in the grand chess match that unfolds.

This intellectual capacity transcends the physicality of the game, elevating basketball from a mere athletic contest to a cerebral engagement. Players transform into mental tacticians, coaches into strategic architects, and recruiters into visionary strategists as they master the art of reading and responding to cascades.

Conceptualize. Your thoughts?

Intellect and the Dynamics of the Game:

At the heart of reading the opponent's cascades lies the profound influence of intellect on the game's dynamics. Basketball, in its essence, is not merely a test of physical prowess; it is a mental duel where the intellect shapes the ebb and flow of play. The strategic decisions made on the court, whether to press aggressively, execute a pick-and-roll, or adapt defensive strategies, are a manifestation of intellectual acuity.

The intersection of intellect and cascades becomes a crucible where players refine their decision-making skills. A player with a keen intellect doesn't just react; they anticipate. They read the subtle cues, recognize patterns, and discern the opponent's intentions before they unfold. This elevated level of play requires mental agility that transforms the player into a maestro, orchestrating the movements on the court.

Conceptualize. Your thoughts?

A Symphony of Strategic Play:

As we delve deeper, the connection between intellect and cascades unfolds as a symphony of strategic play. Skilled players, through their intellectual mastery, disrupt negative cascades and exploit opponents' weaknesses. The court becomes a canvas, and each move is a stroke of strategic brilliance, contributing to the evolving narrative of the game.

Consider a scenario where a player, recognizing the opponent's tendency to collapse on defense, exploits this cascade by delivering pinpoint passes to open teammates. The extended exploration of such strategic maneuvers reveals how intellect becomes a beacon, guiding players to manipulate the cascades in their favor. This symphony of strategic play extends beyond individual brilliance to the harmonious coordination of the entire team, where each player contributes to the orchestration of success.

Conceptualize. Your thoughts?

Reflections on Decision-Making:

The exploration of reading opponents' cascades serves as a mirror, urging players, coaches, and recruiters to reflect on the profound influence of their decisions. Deciphering opponents' moves is not just about reacting in the moment; it's about making decisions that influence the course of the game. This reflective pause becomes an opportunity for self-awareness and a deeper understanding of the strategic implications of every move.

Players, in their pursuit of excellence, are encouraged to go beyond immediate action and consider the long-term consequences of their decisions. Coaches, as strategic architects, reflect on how their decisions shape the cascades that unfold on the court. Recruiters, with a visionary lens, reflect on the potential of players to read and respond to opponent cascades, recognizing the intellectual prowess that goes beyond physical skill.

Conceptualize. Your thoughts?

Player's Mastery on the Court:

The extended exploration of reading opponents' cascades places the player's mastery on the court under a magnifying glass. It goes beyond highlight-reel dunks and pinpoint three-pointers, shedding light on the player's cognitive prowess. The court, seen through the lens of cascades, becomes a canvas where players paint strategic masterpieces with every dribble, pass, and defensive play.

Consider a player who, through intellectual acuity, anticipates an opponent's offensive set and intercepts a crucial pass. The player's mastery is not confined to physical agility but extends to mental sharpness. This extended narrative becomes a celebration of players who transcend athleticism, embodying a holistic mastery that includes both physical prowess and intellectual finesse.

Conceptualize. Your thoughts?

Coach's Strategic Artistry:

The exploration extends to the sideline, where coaches, in their strategic artistry, read opponents' cascades like seasoned chess grandmasters. A coach's decisions, from calling timeouts to designing plays, are not arbitrary; they are strategic moves in response to the cascades unfolding on the court. The sideline transforms into a command center where the coach, armed with intellect, influences the game's destiny.

The coach's role as a strategic architect is illuminated as we dissect scenarios where a timely substitution disrupts an opponent's momentum or a well-devised play capitalizes on observed cascades. The extended narrative becomes an homage to coaches who, with their strategic acumen, guide their teams through the labyrinth of cascades, shaping victories and learning from defeats.

Conceptualize. Your thoughts?

Recruiter's Visionary Strategist:

In the grand tapestry of basketball, recruiters emerge as visionary strategists. Their ability to read and assess a player's capacity to understand opponents' cascades becomes a key factor in talent acquisition. Beyond the physical attributes, recruiters seek players with the intellectual agility to contribute to the strategic landscape of the game.

Consider a recruiter identifying a player with an innate ability to read and respond to opponents' cascades, envisioning how this skill will enhance the team's overall dynamics. The extended exploration underscores the importance of recruiters as architects of team strategy, recognizing the intellectual dimension that players bring to the game.

Conceptualize. Your thoughts?

The Interconnected Web of Intellect and Cascades:

In the intricate dance of basketball strategy, the web of intellect and cascades emerges as interconnected strands shaping the destiny of the game. The player's mastery, the coach's strategic artistry, and the recruiter's visionary perspective become nodes in this intricate network. Each decision, each move, is a pulsating point in this web, creating a collective intelligence that defines the course of play.

Consider a team where players, coached by a strategic mastermind, execute plays with the precision of a well-tuned instrument. The recruiter's vision of assembling a roster with diverse intellectual capacities becomes the foundation for success. The extended narrative becomes a testament to the collaborative intelligence that transcends individual brilliance, elevating the team to a realm where intellect and cascades intertwine seamlessly.

Conceptualize. Your thoughts?

Lessons Beyond the Court:

As the exploration of reading opponents' cascades unfolds, the lessons extend beyond the boundaries of the basketball court. Intellectual acuity, decision-making process, and strategic insight cultivated in the crucible of the game become life skills. Players, coaches, and recruiters carry these lessons into the broader arena of life, where the ability to read and respond to cascades applies to diverse challenges.

Consider a player applying the strategic thinking honed on the court to navigate complex decisions in their personal or professional life. The coach's ability to read cascades becomes a metaphor for leadership, guiding teams through the dynamics of change. The recruiter's visionary perspective extends beyond the basketball arena, recognizing potential in varied contexts.

Conceptualize. Your thoughts?

The Legacy of Intellect and Cascades:

In the concluding notes of this exploration, the legacy of intellect and cascades becomes apparent

Conceptualize. Your thoughts?

CHAPTER 3
HOW THE GAME IS BEING LEARNED

THE SCIENTIFIC DESCRIPTION of memes centers around the concept of cultural transmission through imitation and variation, a theory first introduced by British evolutionary biologist Richard Dawkins in his 1976 book "The Selfish Gene." The term "meme" is derived from a shortening of the Greek word "meme," meaning "that which is imitated," and Dawkins used it to describe an idea. Behavior, style, or usage that spreads from person to person within a culture.

Conceptualize. Your thoughts?

:OR:

In scientific terms, memes are analogous to genes in that they self-replicate, mutate, and respond to selective pressures. However, unlike genes which are biological units of heredity, memes are cultural units of transmission. They propagate themselves in the meme pool—the sum total of all memes in a culture-by leaping from brain to brain via a process that, in the broadest sense, can be called imitation. In short, you play like who you play with or coach by, like who you watch, and your style of play is affected by your environment. (Janus Sanders)

Let's break down the science of memes in a way that hits home for us on the court. Here's a playbook on how memes work, and trust me, it's not just about funny cat videos.

1. Replication: Dunk Like You Mean It.

Just like you work on replicating that perfect dunk, memes replicate by being shared and communicated among players and coaches.

Does your killer move? They get shared on the court.

2. Variation: Mix It Up

Like a crossover, memes change and mutate over time. Just like you change your crossover to keep defenders on their toes, memes evolve as they spread.

The more variation, the more attention they grab.

3. Selection: Game-winning shots

Oh, not all memes are spread equally, just like not all plays are game-winners. There's a natural selection where the most appealing and resonant memes (or plays) are the ones that get shared the most.

Nail that buzzer-beater!

4. Retention: Make It Unforgettable

Oh, successful memes stick around, becoming part of the culture. Think of them like legendary plays in basketball history.

Your unforgettable moves? They're the ones everyone talks about.

5. Transmission: Pass It On, Court to Court

Memes spread through communication and social interaction. Just like passing on the court, memes get shared through speech, writing, and even tech.

Share your moves, pass the ball, and watch the magic happen.

6. Cultural Fitness: Suit Up for Success

Oh, memes that fit well in their environment spread more effectively. It's like your skills fit perfectly into a game strategy.

Stay responsive to the court's climate and innovations, just like memes adapt to their cultural surroundings.

7. Cognitive Neuroscience: Training Your Basketball Brain

Oh, from a neurological perspective, memes are like brain patterns that get processed and transmitted. Your basketball brain processes moves, strategies, and plays, forming patterns that other players pick up on.

It's like a neural slam dunk.

8. Sociology and Anthropology: Hoops Culture

Oh, in these disciplines, memes are studied for their role in social systems. On the court, it's about understanding the role of players, rituals, and the evolution of basketball culture. It's the anthropology of hoops.

So, next time you're out on the court, remember that you're not just playing basketball. You're creating on-court memes that spread through the basketball community. Keep innovating, stay in the game, and let your basketball memes grow.

Conceptualize. Your thoughts?

THE LANGUAGE OF BASKETBALL. **Just like any language, it has its own set of "phonemes" – distinct sounds that carry specific meanings on the court.**

Game Conceptualization: The game isn't just a series of moves; it's a conceptual journey. Think of it like building a language through skills. Coaching and teaching. But here's the catch – many stay in the conceptual realm, ignoring the fundamental building blocks. It's time to open our minds and see the game from various angles.

Sounds of the Game – Our Phonemes: Now, let's imagine every sound during a basketball game as a form of language. It's a bit out there but bear with me. Each sound becomes a phoneme of the "Game," carrying a unique meaning within the sporting event. It's like

Decoding the game through its sounds:

.

Bouncing ball: This rhythmic sound sets the pace of the game, much like phonemes determine the pace of spoken words. It's the heartbeat of the court.

.

Shoe Squeaks: Quick movements or changes in direction are signaled by these squeaks. Just as phonemes shift in language, squeaks shift the dynamics of the game.

.

Grunt or Shout: Reflecting effort or emotion, these sounds mirror how phonemes express complex emotional states in spoken language. It's raw, unfiltered expression on the court.

.

Whistle Blows: Think of whistles as punctuation marks, signaling the end of play or a call for attention. They're the full stops and exclamation marks of the game.

.

Language of the Court: Now, players, coaches, and seasoned spectators aren't just watching; they're understanding this language intuitively. It's a communication system unique to the court. These sounds become our basketball vocabulary.

.

Learning Through Sound: Sure, it might sound a bit creative, but let's not mistake it for the foundations of phonemes in linguistics. The sounds in basketball convey information, but they lack the strict rules and distinctiveness of true phonemes. It's an analogy that adds a layer to the game's complexity. So, as you hit the court, listen to the language it speaks. Every bounce, squeak, grunt, and whistle tells a story. It's not just a game; it's a symphony of sounds, and understanding them takes your basketball IQ to a whole new level on the court and in harmony, "But does it?"

Picture this: A jam-packed gym, the rhythmic squeak of sneakers reverberating off the walls, and every player synced to the beat of the game—a language spoken not with words, but with moves on the court. Now, let's unravel the language of basketball through a tale of phonemes, the smallest units of sound that play ball with concepts familiar to us in the basketball world.

Conceptualize. Your thoughts?

Phonetics - The Fundamentals: Think of phonetics as the fundamental playbook of Basketball. Just as it deals with sound production, it mirrors the nitty-gritty mechanics of the game—the perfect shooting form, defensive reads, and the ball's trajectory. Breaking down the game like a linguist dissecting sounds from stance to grip, akin to articulatory phonetics.

Phonology - The Playbook: Now, imagine phonology as our language's playbook. It's about how sounds interact, creating schemes for effective communication on the court. It's your strategy—when to cut, when to set a pick, when to spot up for the jumper. It's the function and patterning of sounds in speech, just like the plays that unfold strategically.

Speech Production and Articulation - The Physiology: Tighten those shoelaces; we're delving into the physiology of the game. The systems used to speak parallel the muscle groups needed for that flawless no-look pass or post-footwork. The brain, much like the point guard, orchestrates plays, ensuring the team moves in fluid motion.

Psycholinguistics - The Mind Game: Enter the mind game—psycholinguistics. This field examines language processing, much like how players absorb the ins and outs of the game. From rookies picking up plays to veterans reading the defense, mental preparation and in-game decision-making embody psycholinguistics in action.

Neurolinguistics - The Command Center: Now, meet the command center—the brain on the sidelines, the coach. Study the zone, grasp the match's flow, and anticipate your opponent's next move—this echoes neurolinguistics exploring the brain's role in language tasks. In essence, understanding the scientific facets of phonemes draws a parallel to the fundamentals of basketball—clear communication, precision, strategy, thought processing, and the pivotal brain-behind-the-operation view that encapsulates the game we live for. Much like linguistics dissects language for clarity and function, basketball players and enthusiasts break down plays to maximize efficiency and dominate the court.

So, let's take this understanding and turn it into a victory on the hardwood!

"The Language of Basketball" embarks on an insightful journey by analogizing the sounds of basketball to linguistic phonemes. This research paper explores the profound parallels drawn between the language of the game and the foundational concepts of phonemes in linguistic theory. By delving into the nuanced meanings carried by distinct sounds during a basketball game.

We aim to unravel the intricate layers of communication on the court. This chapter's imaginative approach, conceptualizing every sound as a "phoneme of the game," not only enriches the understanding of basketball's complexity but also fosters the development of a unique and expressive basketball vocabulary among players, coaches, and spectators.

Conceptualize. Your thoughts?

II. Analogy Between Basketball Language and Phonemes, Linguistic

Foundations Phonetic

Analogies:

Drawing inspiration from linguistic theory, this section establishes the foundational analogies between the sounds of basketball and phonemes. We delve into the fundamental principles of phonetics, dissecting how the sounds produced on the court mirror the articulatory processes that linguists study. This exploration lays the groundwork for understanding the intricate relationship between the language of basketball and the phonetic nuances inherent in spoken languages.

Theoretical Underpinnings:

The chapter's analogy between basketball language and phonemes is grounded in linguistic theory. We examine the theoretical underpinnings that support the comparison, showcasing how the study of phonemes can be extended beyond traditional language to encapsulate the unique auditory landscape of the basketball court. This theoretical framework illuminates the creative lens through which we interpret the soundscape of the game.

Imagining Every Sound as a "Phoneme of the Game" Conceptual Framework Basketball as a Sonic Landscape:

This subsection explores the conceptualization of basketball as a sonic landscape where every sound becomes a "phoneme of the game." By reframing the auditory elements of the sport as linguistic units, we elevate the significance of each sound, transforming the court into a canvas of expressive communication. Players, coaches, and spectators are invited to perceive the game through a lens that transcends mere physical actions, adding depth to the basketball experience.

Creativity in Interpretation:

Imagining every sound as a "phoneme of the game" encourages a creative approach to interpretation. Players, coaches, and spectators are prompted to develop a unique basketball vocabulary, infusing the game with personalized meanings and expressions. This creativity enhances the overall experience, fostering a deeper connection to the sport and contributing to the richness of basketball culture.

Conceptualize. Your thoughts?

Development of a Unique Basketball Vocabulary Expressive Communication Player-Coach-Spectator Dynamics:

The development of a unique basketball vocabulary becomes a dynamic process involving players, coaches, and spectators. This section dissects the interactions between these three entities, highlighting how the shared understanding of sounds as "phonemes of the game" creates a symbiotic language. The evolving dialogue on the court reflects the collaborative construction of a basketball lexicon that resonates with shared meanings.

Enhancing Understanding:

The creative approach to developing a unique basketball vocabulary contributes to a heightened understanding of the game's complexity. Players can communicate more efficiently on the court, coaches can convey strategies with nuanced precision, and spectators can engage with the sport on a deeper level. This section explores the cognitive and emotional dimensions of enhanced understanding facilitated by the imaginative framing of basketball sounds as linguistic phonemes.

Exploration of the language of basketball as an analogy to linguistic phonemes unveils a new dimension in the comprehension of the sport. By imagining every sound as a "phoneme of the game," players, coaches, and spectators are invited to partake in a creative, expressive dialogue that transcends the physical actions on the court. The development of a unique basketball vocabulary becomes a collaborative endeavor, enriching the cultural tapestry of the sport.

This research paper invites readers to appreciate basketball not only as a physical game but as a linguistic and artistic endeavor where the sounds of the game contribute to a shared narrative that resonates beyond the boundaries of the court. In essence, understanding the scientific facets of phonemes draws a parallel to the fundamentals of basketball—clear communication, precision, strategy, thought processing, and the pivotal brain-behind-the-operation view that encapsulates the game we live for. Much like linguistics dissects language for clarity and function, basketball players and enthusiasts break down plays to maximize efficiency and dominate the court.

Conceptualize. Your thoughts?

CHAPTER 5
HARMONY

OF FAITH AND REASON, the intersection of God's timing and cognitive science in the pursuit of basketball endeavors, is a profound and thought-provoking topic that delves into the deeper relationship between faith and reason. The cognitive processes involved in decision-making, combined with spiritual discernment, create a harmonious blend that shapes paths and decisions in the game of basketball.

When we look at the correlation between faith and reason in the context of basketball, we are invited to reflect on the profound influence of decisions and the lasting impact they can have on the game. This exploration of the intersection serves as a bridge, connecting the spiritual realm with the cognitive sciences and unraveling the intricate dance of faith and reason. At the heart of this exploration is the concept of timing – God's timing, to be precise. The notion that there is divine timing at play in the realm of basketball is both captivating and insightful. It prompts us to contemplate the significance of each moment on the court and how it aligns with a greater cosmic order.

Furthermore, the interplay between God's timing and the cognitive processes involved in decision-making opens up a rich tapestry of possibilities for understanding the game at a deeper level. The cognitive processes involved in decision-making, such as perception, attention, memory, and judgment, are fundamental to the way basketball players navigate the game.

These processes are intertwined with the discernment of timing and opportunities—a spiritual element that speaks to the faith-driven aspect of decision-making on the court. This interweaving of cognitive processes with spiritual discernment underscores the complexity of the human experience and the multifaceted nature of decision-making in basketball.

Moreover, the harmonious blend of faith and reason extends beyond the individual player and encompasses the dynamics of teamwork and collaboration. The ability to synchronize cognitive processes with spiritual discernment within a team setting speaks to the transformative power of collective faith and reason. As players synergize their cognitive abilities with spiritual alignment, they create a unified force that transcends mere physical skill, elevating the game to a higher plane of interconnectedness.

Within this context, the exploration of the intersection between God's timing and cognitive science sheds light on the interconnectedness of faith and reason. It prompts us to consider the role of divine guidance in decision-making and how it intersects with the cognitive pathways that shape our perceptions and choices.

This contemplation invites readers to delve into the depths of human consciousness and the interplay between the spiritual and the rational in the context of basketball endeavors. As we delve deeper into the harmonious blend of faith and reason, it becomes evident that this intersection holds far-reaching implications beyond the confines of the basketball court. The interplay between faith and reason influences not only individual decisions but also the collective ethos of teams, organizations, and communities. It fosters a culture of mindfulness, where the alignment of cognitive processes with spiritual discernment becomes a guiding principle for navigating life's challenges and opportunities.

The exploration of this intersection also encompasses the ethical dimension of decision-making in basketball and beyond. The integration of faith and reason prompts an introspective examination of the motivations behind our choices and the moral implications of our actions. It challenges us to approach decision-making with a depth of awareness that extends beyond mere analytical reasoning, calling for holistic discernment that considers the spiritual and ethical dimensions of our choices.

Intriguingly, the harmonious blend of faith and reason in the pursuit of basketball endeavors opens up a dialogue that transcends cultural, religious, and philosophical boundaries. It invites individuals from diverse backgrounds to engage in a contemplative exploration of the universal themes of timing, decision-making, and the interplay between the spiritual and the cognitive. This inclusive dialogue fosters a sense of interconnectedness and shared understanding, transcending differences to uncover the common threads that bind humanity together.

As we ponder the intricate dance of faith and reason in the context of basketball, we are compelled to recognize the inherent beauty of this harmonious blend. It serves as a testament to the depth and complexity of the human experience, transcending the dichotomy of spiritual versus rational and embracing the interconnectedness of these seemingly divergent facets of human consciousness.

Furthermore, the exploration of this intersection challenges us to reframe our perspectives on decision-making, inviting us to consider the interplay between intuition and analysis, faith and reason, and the dynamic interweaving of these elements in shaping our experiences on and off the court. It prompts us to embrace a more holistic approach to decision-making, one that honors the intricate dance of cognitive processes and spiritual discernment. At the core of this exploration lies the recognition that the pursuit of basketball endeavors is not merely a physical and intellectual pursuit but a profound journey of self-discovery and spiritual growth.

It calls upon players, coaches, and enthusiasts to embark on a quest for deeper understanding, to seek alignment between faith and reason, and to recognize the transformative power of this harmonious blend in shaping the game and, by extension, our lives. In conclusion, the exploration of the intersection between God's timing and cognitive science in the pursuit of basketball endeavors offers a lens through which we can contemplate the profound interplay of faith and reason. It encourages a reflective exploration of the spiritual and cognitive dimensions of decision-making, inviting us to recognize the harmonious blend that shapes our paths and decisions on the court and beyond.

This exploration serves as a reminder of the interconnectedness of the human experience and the transformative power of aligning faith and reason in the pursuit of excellence.

Conceptualize. Your thoughts?

CHAPTER 6

THE BASKETBALL MEME POOL - A SYMPHONY OF REPLICATION, MUTATION, AND SELECTIVE PRESSURES

IN THE DYNAMIC realm of basketball, the concept of the "meme pool" pulsates with life, shaped by the interplay of replication, mutation, and selective pressures. This extended exploration not only dissects the active role of players in contributing to this rich meme pool but also delves deeper into the nuanced mechanisms of cultural transmission within the sport.

Conceptualize. Your thoughts?

Players as Architects of the Meme Pool:

Far from being a static stage, the basketball court transforms into an arena where players actively shape the meme pool. This isn't a passive assimilation of moves but a dynamic process where players consciously or inadvertently contribute to the cultural fabric of the sport. The echoes of iconic moves resonate through the hardwood, creating a living tapestry where basketball's history and innovation intertwine.

Memetic Mutations Unveiled:

As we explore the concept of memetic mutations, the basketball court emerges as a canvas where strategies undergo a constant evolution. No longer confined to rigid plays, basketball becomes a dynamic landscape where players, like creative alchemists, introduce variations and innovative strategies. This expanded understanding challenges the traditional notion of basketball as a static entity, revealing it as a living, breathing narrative shaped by the adaptive mutations within the meme pool.

Conceptualize. Your thoughts?

Selective Pressures: Shaping the Basketball Culture:

The forces influencing basketball culture come under the spotlight as we dissect the concept of selective pressure. Moves, strategies, or plays aren't arbitrary; they endure and evolve based on their effectiveness within the cultural context. This section sheds light on the delicate balance between tradition and innovation, showcasing how the enduring elements of basketball culture are subject to the selective pressures exerted by their impact on the game.

The Player's Role in Cultural Transmission:

The player, once viewed merely as an executor of plays, emerges as a crucial agent in the cultural transmission of basketball knowledge. This expanded exploration scrutinizes how players become conduits for the perpetuation of the sport's essence. The court is no longer a passive stage; it's a dynamic platform where the collective basketball wisdom is transmitted, ensuring that the echoes of iconic moves resonate across generations.

Conceptualize. Your thoughts?

Replicating Moves and Plays:

Within the player's role in cultural transmission, the act of replicating moves and plays becomes a focal point. Players, consciously or instinctively, carry the torch of the basketball legacy. From the flawless execution of a jump shot reminiscent of basketball legends to the artful replication of iconic defensive maneuvers, the player becomes a custodian of the sport's cultural DNA. The court becomes a living archive where the past seamlessly merges with the present.

Varying Strategies: Injecting Diversity into the Meme Pool:

Beyond replication, players become architects of diversity within the meme pool by introducing varying strategies. The creativity injected into the game through unique approaches becomes a testament to the sport's resilience and adaptability. The extended exploration underscores that the evolution of basketball is not a monolithic process; it thrives on the diverse strategies injected into the meme pool, ensuring that the sport remains a vibrant narrative.

Conceptualize. Your thoughts?

A Pivotal Conclusion:

With an exploration into the profound implications of the scientific concept of memes for the cultural fabric of basketball. The dynamic interplay of replication, mutation, and selective pressures within the meme pool reshapes our understanding of basketball as a living entity. The player's active contribution to the cultural transmission of basketball knowledge transforms the sport into a vibrant, ever-changing narrative.

Reflecting on Basketball as a Cultural Phenomenon:

This extended research incentives readers to reflect on basketball not merely as a game but as a cultural phenomenon. Once seen as a space for athletic prowess, the basketball court becomes a stage where knowledge is disseminated, mutated, and perpetuated through the intricate dance of memes within the unique meme pool of basketball culture. This reflection is an invitation to witness the continuous evolution of the sport, appreciating its dynamic nature and embracing the symbiotic relationship between players and the ever-changing basketball meme pool. In summary, basketball is not frozen in time; it is a living, breathing entity shaped by the contributions of players who actively engage with the meme pool, leaving an indelible mark on the sport's cultural landscape. This exploration serves as a guide for enthusiasts, players, and scholars alike, providing a lens through which to appreciate the richness and complexity of basketball's cultural evolution.

Unveiling the Symphony of Basketball

As I lace up my sneakers and reflect on this transformative journey, I'm compelled to share not just a conclusion but an anthem, a hymn that intertwines the spiritual rhythm of basketball with the engineering precision that defines our physical and intellectual prowess. Whether you're a court maestro, a strategic architect, or an insatiable thirst for understanding, let's explore the cadence and intricacies that propel basketball beyond a game into a divine symphony.

The Artistry of Action Cascades: A Divine Choreography

In the sacred realm of the court, every dribble, every pivot, is an offering—a testament to the divine choreography of action cascades. Imagine the court as a celestial canvas, where each move is a brushstroke guided by an unseen hand. As athletes, we're not just players but instruments, harmonizing with the cosmic forces that shape the destiny of the game. Let's delve deeper into this divine dance, acknowledging the Higher Power orchestrating the cascades that define our journey on the hardwood.

Conceptualize. Your thoughts?

Intellectual Prowess: An Engineering Marvel

In the symphony of basketball, the intellect becomes the engineering marvel that transcends mere strategy. It's the blueprint of plays etched by the Almighty's hand—a celestial algorithm guiding us through the dynamic chessboard of the court. As athletes, coaches, and engineers of the game, we recognize that our mental acuity is a divine gift. Let's unravel the intricate design of plays, understanding that our minds are instruments tuned to the divine frequencies that govern the court's sacred geometry.

The basketball meme Pool: Cultural Icons in Divine Tapestry

As we navigate the basketball meme pool, let's envision it as a sacred tapestry woven by the hands of the Divine Artist. Every move, every strategy, is a stroke of genius painted onto the canvas of basketball culture. The echoes of iconic plays resonate not just with the cheers of fans but with the celestial applause of the Creator. In exploring this cultural odyssey, we acknowledge that we're custodians of a divine legacy, contributing our chapters to the eternal story written in the celestial script of the game.

Athletes as Divine Messengers: Cultural Transmission through Divine Echoes

In the continuum of cultural transmission, athletes emerge as divine messengers, carrying the torch of basketball knowledge bestowed upon us by a Higher Source. The court becomes a pulpit where we preach not just athleticism but values embedded in the divine language of the game. Our role transcends the physical; we're conduits for divine messages encrypted in every dribble, every pass, and every dunk. Let's celebrate our divine responsibility as athletes, understanding that our influence echoes through the annals of basketball history.

A Divine Symphony: The Essence of Basketball

Imagine the court as a sacred altar where athletes, coaches, and fans gather to witness a divine symphony. Every move, every play, is a note in this celestial composition. As we conclude this divine journey, let's not bid farewell but express gratitude for the divine privilege of engaging in this cosmic dance. The lessons from basketball extend beyond the court, becoming hymns for life—a testament to our divine capacity for growth, resilience, and unity.

Conceptualize. Your thoughts?

A Divine Blessing: Navigating Life's Court

As we part ways, may we carry the spirit of the game onto the courts of our lives. Just as we acknowledge the divine presence on the basketball court, let's recognize the Almighty's guidance on life's journey. The symphony of basketball is but a prelude to the grand orchestration of our existence. As athletes, engineers, and divine beings, let's approach every aspect of life with the same awareness, respect, and integrity that we bring to the game.

A Divine Encore: The Tale Continues

In this divine narrative, our paths may diverge, but the tale continues. Every dribble, every shot, is a divine encore—a promise that the symphony of basketball plays on. Until we reconvene on the sacred hardwood, may the Almighty bless our journeys, both on and off the court. As we part ways, let the echoes of this divine symphony resonate in your hearts, and may you find divine inspiration at every step of your journey.

Amen

ABOUT THE AUTHOR

Louis A. Barham III, the author of *Symphony of the Game*, is an experienced executive and former athlete with a rich background in leadership and sports. He has held key roles in numerous organizations, guiding them towards success by creating and implementing strategic visions, leading executive teams, and ensuring operational excellence in both the USA and Canada. His leadership skills extend to overseeing operations, evaluating organizational success, and representing his organizations in various civic and professional activities.

Louis's journey includes a distinguished athletic career. As a student-athlete, he excelled in basketball, winning several awards and recognitions. He played for Keyano College, where he led his team to their first CCAA National Championships, earning a final national ranking of #8. His accolades include multiple ACAC All-Conference awards, Huskies Athlete of the Year, and the prestigious Brent Butt Award for leadership and community involvement.

In addition to his athletic achievements, Louis has a proven track record in executive leadership. He has served as a CEO, leading organizations through strategic planning and implementation, guiding executive leaders, and fostering a learning environment for continued growth and success. His commitment to leadership and community is reflected in his active participation in industry events and associations, enhancing both his skills and his organization's reputation.

Louis's multifaceted experience and dedication to excellence make him a dynamic leader capable of driving the growth of any organization